LOOK AT
TEETH

Franklin Watts
12a Golden Square
London W1R 4AB

Franklin Watts Australia
14 Mars Road
Lane Cove
N.S.W. 2066

ISBN 0 86313 697 4

Design: David Bennett
Illustrations: Simon Roulstone
Editor: Ruth Thomson

The author and publisher would like
to thank the following for their
participation in the photography
for this book:
Lisa Rukin, Harriet Chanarin, Liz, Sam
and Joe London; Solveig, Ezra, Zachary
and Elisabeth Emerson; Neil, Leo and
Chloe Thomson; Robert Chapman, Alexandra
Cragg, Nicola Hickman-Robertson and
Veronica Green.

False teeth supplied courtesy of
Ballons, London.

Additional Photographs
Science Photo Library p9.
Zefa p6, 16
Chris Fairclough p24, 25

Printed in Italy
by G. Canale & C. S.p.A. Turin

LOOK AT
TEETH

Henry Pluckrose

Photography by Mike Galletly

FRANKLIN WATTS
London · New York · Sydney · Toronto

Do you ever look at teeth?

New-born babies have no teeth.
Their teeth have not yet come
through the gums.

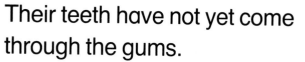

As babies grow,
their teeth appear.
Babies need teeth
to eat solid foods.

By the age of three,
children have a complete set
of 20 baby teeth.

When children are about six,
the baby teeth begin to loosen and fall out.
Permanent teeth grow in their place.

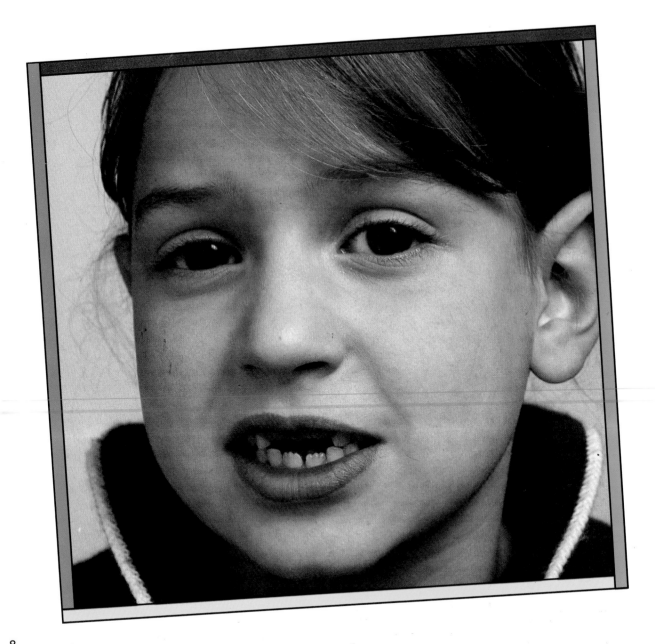

This is an X-ray of a jaw.
Can you see the teeth?

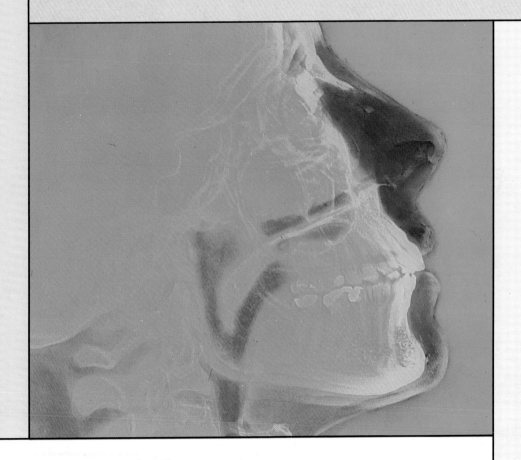

When you are grown up,
you will have 32 teeth –
16 in the upper jaw
and 16 in the lower jaw.

Human beings have four kinds of teeth.
The eight teeth at the front of the mouth
are incisors.
They are used for cutting and slicing food.

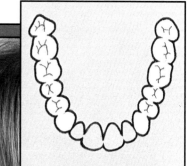

The pointed teeth on either side
of the incisors are called canine teeth.
They are used for tearing food.

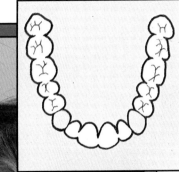

The big teeth at the back of the mouth are called premolars and molars.
They crush and grind food into tiny pieces, so that it is easy to swallow.

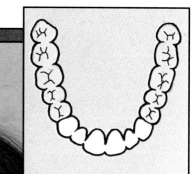

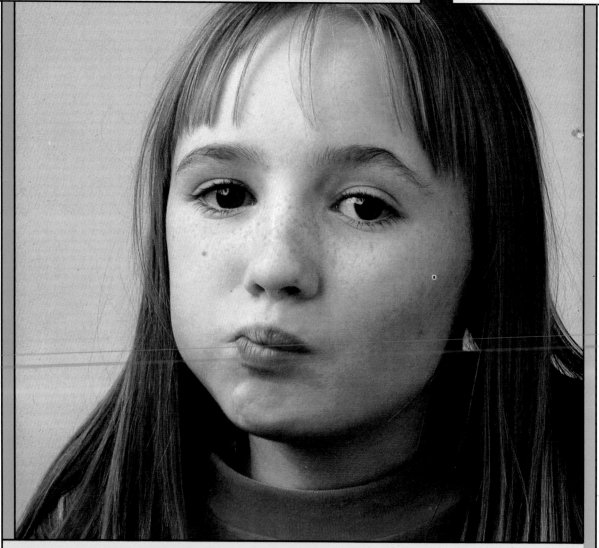

Look at your teeth in a mirror.
Can you see which teeth are the incisors
and which are the canine teeth
and the molars?

Human beings are omnivorous.
They eat all sorts of different things.

Make a list of the foods you eat.
Without incisors, which of these foods
would it be difficult to eat?

Animals have a much simpler diet.
Cats, dogs, lions and tigers are flesh eaters.
They have sharp teeth for tearing flesh.

Sheep, cows and horses eat plants.
They have flatter teeth which can pull up
and chew grasses.

Look how your expression changes
if you alter your teeth!

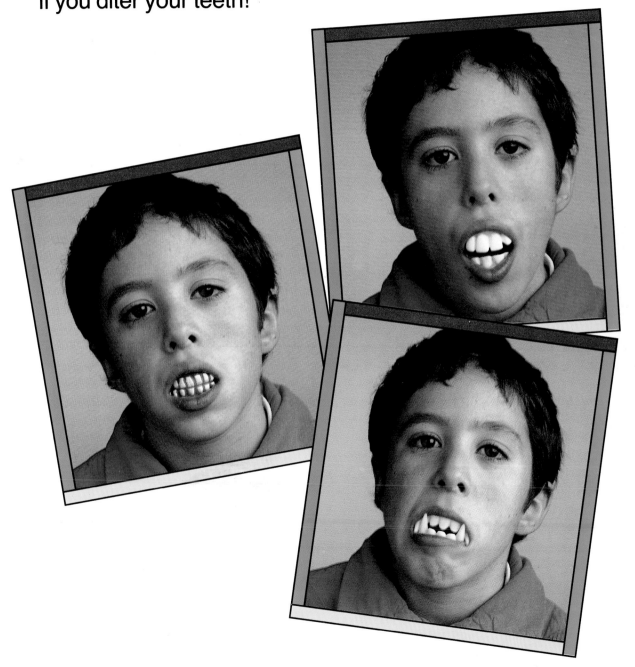

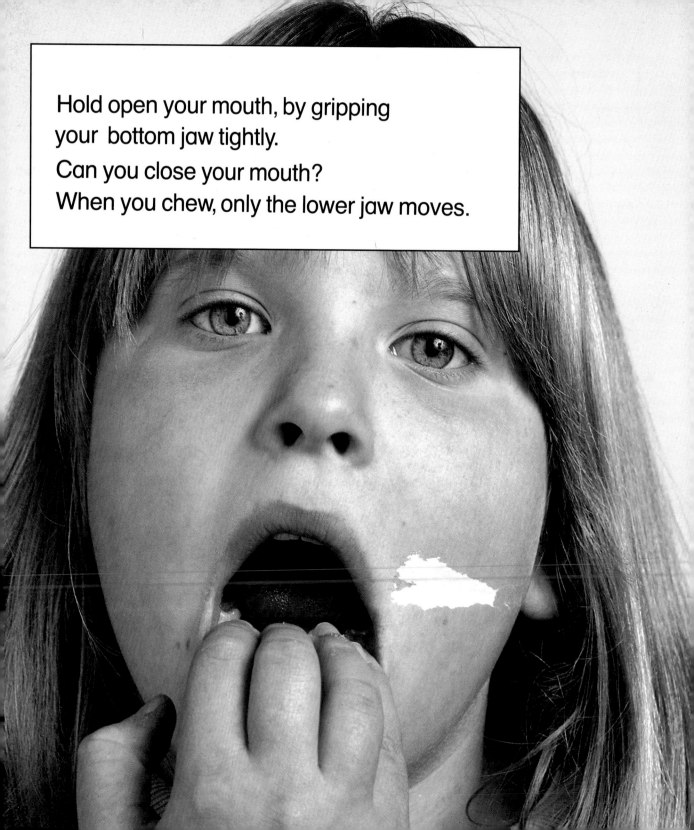

Hold open your mouth, by gripping
your bottom jaw tightly.
Can you close your mouth?
When you chew, only the lower jaw moves.

Your teeth are lubricated with saliva,
which is produced by glands in your face and neck.
Try eating cornflakes without adding any milk.
Are they easy to swallow?

Tiny bits of food stay in your mouth when you eat.
If they are not removed, plaque forms over the teeth.
Plaque is a sticky substance.
It contains billions of bacteria.

The bacteria feed on any tiny scraps of food
left in the mouth.
How much plaque have you got on your teeth?
Use a disclosing tablet to find out.

Plaque collects between the teeth.
It produces an acid which attacks the enamel of the tooth.
Cleaning teeth with a toothbrush and dental floss
helps to remove plaque.

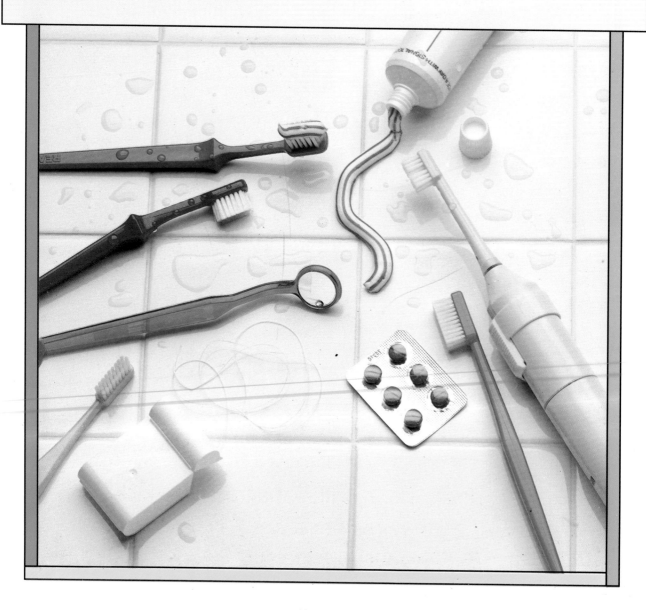

How long do you take to clean your teeth?
Time yourself.

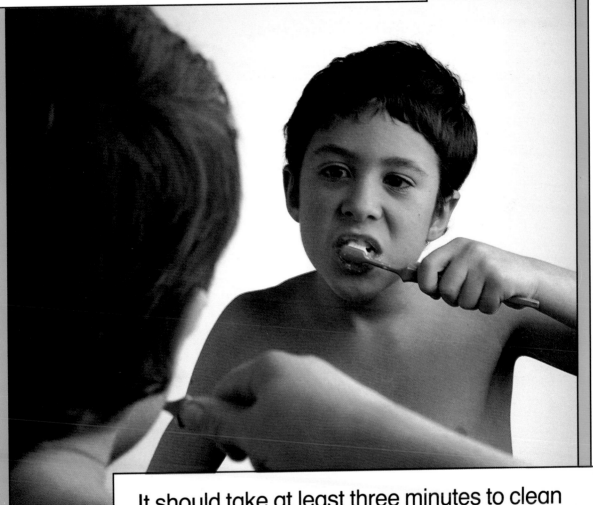

It should take at least three minutes to clean
the whole mouth — the front, the back
and the top of every tooth.
Brush your teeth up and down — never across.

Toothache is usually caused because the enamel of the tooth has been damaged by the acid made by plaque.
The enamel protects the soft centre of the tooth.
A dentist can treat the infected part.

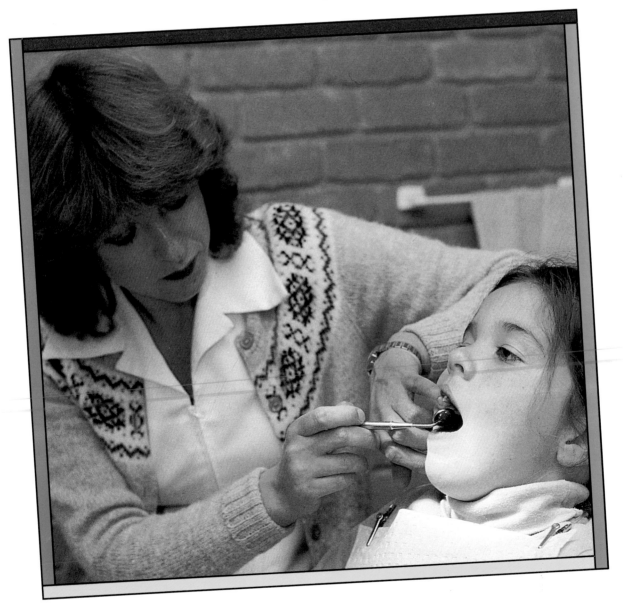

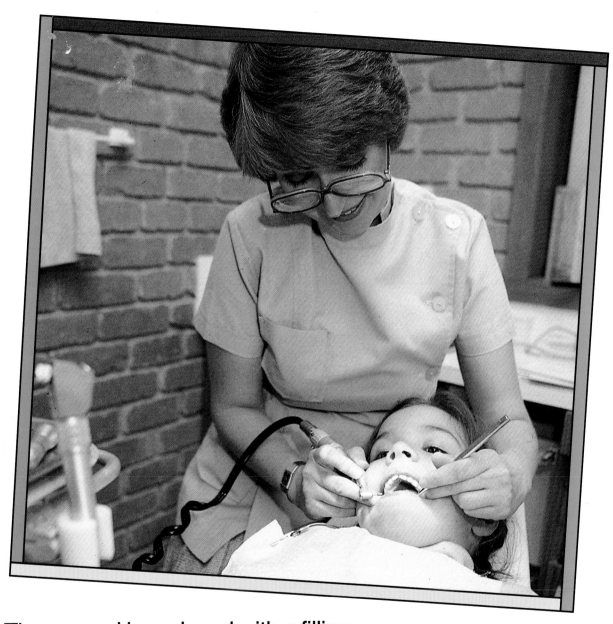

The enamel is replaced with a filling.
The filling is made from a mixture of mercury, silver,
tin, zinc and copper.
It is called amalgam.

Sweet drinks and sugary foods encourage plaque.
By eating foods which contain little sugar (like nuts, fruits
and vegetables), plaque can be reduced.

Which of these foods are bad for your teeth?
Which are best for your teeth?

Teeth can last a lifetime, but only if you care for them. Don't end up with teeth like these!

Do you know?

● Adults have 32 teeth – 16 in the upper jaw and 16 in the lower jaw.

There are 8 incisors, 4 canines, 8 premolars and 12 molars. The last adult teeth to appear are large molars at the very back of the jaw. These do not appear until you are about twenty. They are called wisdom teeth, because they come with age.

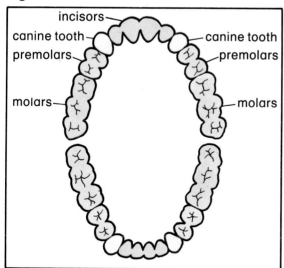

● Teeth are much bigger than you think. The part you can see is called the crown. Under the gum is the root. The root is fixed to the jaw bone.

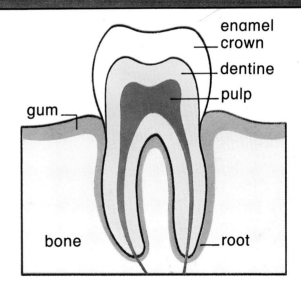

● **The crown** is made of enamel which is hard and white. It protects the tooth from damage.

The dentine beneath the enamel is like bone. It makes up most of the tooth, going right down to the root.

The pulp in the middle is very soft. There are blood vessels and nerves inside it. The nerves enable you to feel heat, cold and pain through the tooth.

● Fluoride is a substance which helps to harden tooth enamel. In some areas, it is added to the water supply. Most toothpastes contain it. Using a fluoride toothpaste is the best way to protect your teeth from decay.

Things to do

● Design a poster to illustrate one or more of these tips for dental health:

1 Visit the dentist for regular check-ups – at least twice a year.

2 Clean your teeth at least twice a day (after breakfast and before you go to bed).

3 Do not eat sweets and sugary foods between meals. Eat fruit, cheese or nuts instead.

4 Drink water rather than a sweetened drink between meals and do not drink sweet drinks just before you go to bed.

5 Eat fewer sweets.

● Do a survey to find out when children lose their baby teeth and gain permanent ones. Which baby teeth do they lose first, second and third?

The first permanent molars come through behind all the baby teeth, without your losing any teeth. You could look in your friends' mouths to see if these molars are through.

● Did you know that having teeth is very necessary for speaking clearly? When you say certain letters, your tongue presses against your teeth. Recite the alphabet very slowly and see if you can discover which letters need the use of your teeth.

● Make a collection of wrappers and labels of different foods and drinks. They will tell you what is in the food and drink. Make a display and a chart to show which foods contain sugar and which ones do not. You may be surprised by some of your findings.

Food	Sugar	No sugar
bread		✔
biscuits	✔	
crisps		✔
fruit yogurt	✔	
nuts		✔

● Collect pictures of animals which either show their teeth or them eating (so that you have a clue of what their teeth are like). Divide them into three groups:

1 Herbivores (animals which live only on plants),

2 Carnivores (which live only on meat)

3 Omnivores (animals which eat both meat and plants)

Find out how birds, which have no teeth, manage to grind their food.

Other words for eating

There are many words which describe different ways of eating. How many of these do you know? Can you mime each one?

bite	gobble	munch
chew	guzzle	crunch
devour	nibble	lick
gnaw	peck	

Sayings about teeth

These are some sayings about teeth. Can you find out what they mean?

To get one's teeth into a problem
To have a sweet tooth
To set one's teeth on edge
To attack with tooth and nail
To be armed to the teeth
To show one's tooth
To be long in the tooth
To cut one's teeth
To gnash one's teeth
To escape by the skin of one's teeth
To demand an eye for an eye and a tooth for a tooth